I0423369

While She Was Sleeping

The Story of Convicted Child Killer Darlie Routier
Specific to the Theory of Repressed Memory of
Childhood Sexual Abuse

An Essay

Brenda Irish Heintzelman

copyright@butterfly publishing, Traverse City, Michigan

No copies, reprints, or electronic transmission or sharing of any portion without author's written permission. Author can be reached at missmensa@gmail.com. This is an opinion essay and is not meant to serve in any way, shape, form, or fashion as medical or legal advice.

For I know the plans I have for you,
to give you a future and a hope.

Jeremiah 29:11

While She Was Sleeping

The Story of Convicted Child Killer Darlie Routier Specific to the Theory of Repressed Memory of Childhood Sexual Abuse

An Essay

There is a convicted child killer sitting on death row in a Texas state prison for over twenty years now who claims she did not murder her children. Her name is Darlie Routier.

On June 6, 1996 at 2:31 a.m. Darlie dialed 911.

00:00.00 "Rowlett 911. What is your emergency".

When the police dispatcher working at the Rowlett, Texas Police Department answered the phone she was shocked by what her caller had to say.

00:01:19 Darlie Routier ...somebody came here...they broke in...
00:03:27 911 Operator #1 ...ma'am?
00:05:11 Darlie Routier ...they just stabbed me and my children...
00:07:16 911 Operator #1 ...what?
00:08:05 Darlie Routier ...they just stabbed me and my kids...my little boys...
00:09:24 911 Operator #1 ...who...who did...
00:11:12 Darlie Routier ...my little boy is dying...

Darlie told the police dispatcher that WHILE SHE WAS SLEEPING an intruder entered her home and fatally stabbed two of her children, Devon and Damon Routier, and that she was also stabbed.

Later Darlie would add to her story and say that WHILE SHE WAS SLEEPING not only did someone stab her and her children but that someone had also removed her panties without her knowing it.

Two minutes after dialing 911 Darlie had still not given her address to the police dispatcher. This is very unusual. Typically when a person is calling for help for their children they very clearly say exactly where their children are located so that help can arrive as soon as possible.

In this case the call was received at a department with a CAD system (computer aided dispatch) which was evidently equipped with both "ALI" and "ANI" (automatic location information and automatic number information). This call was made in 1996 before it became protocol across the country for police dispatchers to confirm the location of the incident in the first few seconds of the call. Nowadays, the dispatcher will confirm location before going into the details of the emergency. However, back in the day, confirmation was not a robotic requirement at all departments.

At the same time, back in the day, when people called for help they would clearly articulate the location of their emergency instead of waiting for the police dispatcher to tell them what to say. In this call however Darlie never mentioned her location and the police dispatcher didn't bother to confirm the location of the emergency until after the first officer had already arrived at the scene.

02:02...Darlie Routier – "Somebody came in while I was sleeping ...me and my little boys were sleeping downstairs... some man ...came in ...stabbed my babies ...stabbed me ...I woke up ...*I was fighting* ...he ran out through the garage ...threw the knife down ...my babies are dying ...they're dead."

Darlie was right, her babies were dead. In fact her son Devon, age six, was probably already dead by the time she dialed 911. Little brother Damon, age five, would soon take his last breath right when the first EMT reached his side just minutes after Darlie finally dialed 911.

Both boys were brutally stabbed while lying on the floor within just a few feet of their mother who claims she was sound asleep on the sofa nearby. She claims that she slept right through it all including being stabbed herself.

But Darlie wasn't stabbed in the same manner that her children were. The children suffered deep penetrating wounds to their vital organs. Not Darlie. In fact her doctor would later testify that Darlie's injuries were "superficial" and could have been self-inflicted.

Notice how quickly Darlie is willing to accept that her children are dead. This isn't normal. Parents cling to the hope their child will survive and have to be torn away from their child in order for emergency crews to perform lifesaving efforts.

Not Darlie. She was on the phone, talking, and talking, and talking about how her children were already dead. She didn't hold her children. She didn't apply pressure to their wounds to help stop the bleeding. She didn't have to be torn away from her children so the EMTs could try to resuscitate them. Because she was in the other room talking on a cordless phone while supposedly checking to see if any of her jewelry had been stolen.

Notice that Darlie told the police dispatcher she fought off the intruder. "I was fighting". This fact would surface later on at her trial when she would deny that she ever said it. It's right there on the audio tape for the jurors to hear. But that didn't stop Darlie from claiming it wasn't really what she had said. Instead, Darlie insisted that during the 911 call she actually said "I was frightening".

I bet she was "frightening" to poor little Devon and Damon Routier.

Just three minutes after Darlie dialed 911 the first responding police officer arrived at the Routier home. He immediately told Darlie to get off the phone and to help her children. She ignored him and kept right on talking.

Then, just thirty seconds after the police officer entered the Routier home, the family dog started barking.

03:30:27 SOUND ...(dog barking)...

This is a very important point and one which serves to show there was never any intruder. The Routier family dog was a known barker who was also known to be very aggressive. In fact, he tried to bite one of the police officers at the scene. Yet, previous to the arrival of the first police officer three minutes after Darlie finally dialed 911, the dog was not barking, at all, ever, not a sound. That means that Darlie's story is hogwash. Obviously had there ever been an intruder as Darlie claimed the dog would have been barking long before the first police officer arrived at the scene.

During her trial on charges of capital murder under cross-examination Darlie admitted that the Routier family dog was a barker. Q. Okay. And that dog you had, he barks a lot at strangers, doesn't he? A. He does bark a lot if he is awake. Q. If he is awake? A. Yes, sir. Q. He is not a real old dog, is he? A. No, I believe he is a couple of years. Q. Okay. I guess he just slept through this whole thing also? A. No, actually I think when everybody started arriving, he was barking.

When everybody started arriving? He was barking when everybody started arriving? But he didn't make a sound when Darlie's imaginary intruder brutally stabbed her children? The dog didn't make a sound when the imaginary intruder attacked her and she was either "fighting" or "frightening". The dog didn't see or hear the intruder? The dog didn't bark at the intruder or bite the intruder? Of course not. Because the intruder never existed except perhaps in Darlie's mind.

At five minutes and nineteen seconds into the call while her children lay dead and dying right before her eyes Darlie suddenly shifted from using the voice tone of a victim saying, "Darin, I promise" to using a very angry tone as she snarled, "Somebody walked in here and did this Darin".

Based on her statement it appears that her husband of almost eight years, Darin Routier, had just accused her of killing their children. Then, as quickly as she changed from sounding like a victim to an incredibly angry woman, she snapped right back to victim mode and said, "It's not because, it's not because, it's not because".

Some transcripts of the 911 call claim that at five minutes and nineteen seconds into the call Darlie said to her husband, "Somebody who did it intentionally walked in here and did it Darin... and then at

05:23:05 Darlie said "There's nothing touched", and again at 05:25:13 "There's nothing touched" followed by "Oh, my God".

Either way it appears evident that her husband accused her of committing the most heinous acts of violence known to womankind. And based on the evidence it appears his first reaction to her intruder story was spot on.

However, from that moment forward, throughout the investigation and the trial anyway, Darin would stand by Darlie's side. It didn't matter what the evidence proved. Darin Routier vowed to stand by Darlie for the rest of their lives and to keep working hard to prove that she was innocent. Except Darin didn't keep his promise. He moved on with his life. He and Darlie divorced and Darin married the woman he had been dating back in 1985 when he and Darlie first met.

Darlie's snarl on the 911 tape probably worked against her in the eyes of the jurors. Hanging on the phone instead of holding her children worked against her at trial as well. And surely the jurors noticed that the dog never barked. But the worst part of Darlie's 911 call was the fact that she seemed to care more about her fingerprints being on the murder weapon than she did about applying pressure to her children's wounds.

05:04:21 Darlie Routier ..."His knife was lying over there and I already picked it up"

05:08:19 911 Operator ...ok ...it's alright ...it's ok...

05:09:20 Darlie Routier ..."God ...I bet if we could have gotten the prints maybe".

Look at how many minutes had already slipped by. Over five minutes after dialing 911 Darlie was still talking on the phone. Her children had died right before her eyes yet she continued to chat on the phone concerning herself with the fingerprints on the murder weapon instead of holding her precious children in her arms and comforting them as they took their last breaths.

Once again, this is simply not normal.

Darlie was normal in one respect though. Well she wasn't but her body was. After the police dispatcher had to tell her twice to get off the phone she finally hung it up and got checked out by one of the EMTs at the crime scene. And the EMT found that Darlie's blood pressure levels and her pulse rate were in fact normal.

What kind of mother would have normal blood pressure levels and a normal pulse rate within minutes of losing two of her children in such a brutal attack? And what kind of mother talks about fingerprints and checks to see if her jewelry is missing instead of actually holding her dying babies in her arms?

A mother who murdered her own children, that's who.

According to one of her closest friends who contacted this author recently, soon after her children were murdered Darlie confessed to killing them. "I did it." Darlie said. "I don't know what happened. I did it".

But just two days after the murders Darlie's story changed. She didn't admit that she did it to the police investigators like she did to her close friend. She went back to the story she told the police dispatcher on the night of the murders. Well at least part of her first story anyway. Darlie stuck with the part about seeing an intruder. That was her story and she was sticking to it. But she didn't claim that she was fighting with the intruder like she did on the 911 call. Instead she said that when she opened her eyes she saw him standing by her feet.

"There was a man standing down at my feet walking away from me". Darlie put her statement in writing for the police investigators. "I walked after him and heard glass breaking. I got halfway through the kitchen and turned back around to run and turn on the light. I ran back towards the utility room and realized there was a big white handled knife laying on the floor. It was then that I realized I had blood all over me and I grabbed the knife thinking he was in the garage. I looked over and saw the door shut to the garage so I thought he might still be in there and I hurried to get Darin. I ran back through the kitchen and realized the entire living area had blood all over everything. I put the knife on the counter and ran into the entrance, turned on a light and started screaming for Darin. I think I screamed twice and he ran out of the bedroom with his jeans on and no glasses and was yelling what is it, what is it. I remember saying he cut them, he tried to kill me, my neck. He ran down the stairs and into the room where the boys were".

At trial her written statement would come back to haunt her. Because the crime scene evidence showed that Darlie's bloody footprints were actually beneath the broken glass as if the glass had fallen to the floor after she said it did and after she had supposedly followed the intruder through the house. And the crime scene evidence would also show that Darlie was not running around right after supposedly opening her eyes and seeing "a man standing down by (her) feet walking away from (her)".

Clearly Darlie was not telling the truth. The direct physical evidence showed that Darlie is the person who murdered her children. And according to one of her closest friends she admitted it.

But what if Darlie actually thinks she is telling the truth when she now says she doesn't remember or she isn't sure or she doesn't know what happened. What if Darlie realized on some level that it must have been her, just as Darin must have realized it too when Darlie was hanging on the phone after she dialed 911, but then she slipped into some sort of denial and has remained in denial ever since?

What if Darlie was having some sort of nightmare when she murdered her children then the trauma of seeing what she had done was too much for her to face?

What if Darlie Routier imagined an intruder standing near feet? What if Darlie Routier truly believed she had slept through the attack on herself and her children and then suddenly came to her senses right before she screamed out for her husband?

What if at some level Darlie realized she is the person who killed her own children but was successful in convincing herself that the intruder in her mind really existed after all?

She told her friend that she "did it". But within two days she went right back to telling the police her intruder story again.

What if Darlie was actually having some sort of nightmare stemming from her claims that she had been sexually molested as a child? What if in her nightmare she was fighting back? What if in real life she was stabbing who she thought was the man she claims had molested her? The same man, by the way, who her mother stayed married to for another ten years. The same man who Darlie had allowed her children to spend the day with just three weeks before they were murdered.

Darlie was not able to give a description of the "intruder" except to say that he wore a baseball cap, he had dark hair, and he was tall. Is the man she has accused of sexually molesting her when she was a little girl known for wearing a baseball cap? Is he tall? But of course, most men do wear baseball caps, and any grown man would seem tall to an eight year old Darlie.

Just eight days after the murders Darlie is seen partying at the cemetery where her children are buried in a shared grave. She is dancing. She is singing. She is laughing. And she is talking non-stop to a reporter about her party and how she believes that Devon and Damon are having a party too.

Clearly she is a woman in denial. But I doubt Darlie's denial skills first appeared when she killed her children. Adult survivors of childhood sexual abuse know how to lie. They know how to pretend. They know how to keep secrets. And looking happy when they're not is a skill they will use for the rest of their lives.

I'm not saying that Darlie was masking some sort of sadness or grief at her party when she was laughing and singing and spraying silly string on her sons' shared grave. I'm saying Darlie learned how to lie at an early age. She learned how to keep secrets. She learned how to pretend. And on that day at the cemetery she was lying. She was keeping secrets. She was pretending because she knew what she did. She knew she had killed her children. She knew they were dead. And she smiled. Perhaps Darlie was smiling because she didn't get caught.

She didn't get caught yet, anyway.

Darlie wasn't the only person at that party who was pretending. Her mother and her husband were too. Her husband had already evidently accused Darlie of killing their children as evidenced by the 911 tape when Darlie suddenly snapped at him and said in an angry voice that "Someone walked in here and did this Darin!" But Darin wasn't the only family member to suspect Darlie was the person who murdered her children. Her own mother admitted later that she said to Darlie, "Is there anything that I should know?" Of course, according to her mother anyway, Darlie supposedly said she saw a man and that she did not murder her children.

"That family is hurting"

After Darlie's trial one of the jurors appeared on the Leeza Gibbons talk show alongside Darlie's mother, also named Darlie, and Darlie's husband Darin. There was also a writer up on the stage and a court watcher. The court watcher summed up the case, and perhaps Darlie's life, beautifully when she told the audience that in her opinion "that family is hurting". The same guest also stated that in her opinion the entire family is in denial.

There is no doubt that family is hurting. The question is how badly was that family hurting before Darlie murdered her children. How many years was that family in denial? How many years had that family been pretending? How many years had that family lied, to themselves, to each other, and to the outside world?

Darin's mom, Sarilda, and Darlie's sister, Dana, were also on the show. Dana was able to speak clearly about how she was the only person who got to say goodbye to the boys. She talked about the supposed vow renewal ceremony that Darlie was planning for almost three years down the road. (Darlie's wedding dress was draped over a chair in the living room and this is the excuse the family gave to the police detectives during the investigation). Dana talked about silly string and how she and her "fiancé" bought a big sign and balloons and brought along the silly string and "poppers" to the party at the cemetery. But when the talk show host asked Dana one simple but evidently very frightening question, Dana burst into tears. The talk show host asked Dana about Darlie's mood just hours before the murders.

"What was your sister's state of mind that night?"

Dana couldn't answer. She sat there and cried. So her mother jumped in and answered the question for her even though Darlie senior wasn't there at the house like Dana was right before the boys were murdered. Darlie senior wasn't the person who was at the house shortly after the murders and who called to say it wasn't just Devon and Damon who were dying but that Darlie was dying too. Darlie's mom wasn't the person who suddenly had to leave the house at nine or nine-thirty at night. But Dana, the person who was right there, who saw Darlie right before she murdered her children, couldn't answer the question about Darlie's state of mind.

In fact, Dana had been living with Darlie and Darin then suddenly, just hours before Devon and Damon were murdered, Dana had to leave. She said later that she couldn't reach her boyfriend and she didn't want him to worry about her so she asked Darin to take her right then and there to her boyfriend's apartment. But obviously, if she couldn't reach her boyfriend then he must not have been too worried about her. And obviously, for her to have to leave suddenly it is quite possible there's a whole lot more to her story.

But she didn't say a word. She sat there while her mother took over and answered the question about Darlie's "state of mind" for her.

Think of that timeline. Dana had been staying with Darlie and Darin. She was just fifteen years old at the time but already had moved out of her mother's house. She spent some time shacking up with her boyfriend at his apartment and some of the time at Darlie and Darin's house. Then suddenly she had to leave Darlie's house at nine or nine-thirty at night. Darin drove her to her boyfriends. He returned home and, according to Darlie's written police statement, he and Darlie "had words". He finally went up the stairs to go to bed without Darlie at 1:00 a.m. And just ninety-one minutes later Darlie dialed 911 and reported that WHILE SHE WAS SLEEPING an intruder had stabbed her and her children.

Dana didn't say a word on the talk show when she was asked about Darlie's state of mind. But she sure spoke up without a problem or any tears falling down her cheeks when she suddenly became angry with the juror who was a guest on the show. By her reaction to the juror it appears that Darlie isn't the only one in the family with a little anger management problem going on.

The juror was answering questions and as she spoke about Darlie's behavior after the murders suddenly Dana jumped right in as if she was auditioning for the roller derby. In a raised voice, and with her finger pointed right at the juror while Dana leaned in for the attack, she suddenly lashed out saying, "Have you ever killed any children? Do you know what situation you'd be in? Do you know how you would be?"

The audience jeered, and rightfully so, while Darlie's family appeared to be oblivious to the absurdity of Dana's words.

Juror – "They were feet away from her head. Feet. That's all, just feet".

Juror - "If my children were feet away from my head the first child may have gotten stabbed but the second one he wouldn't have gotten near without getting through me. (Applause).

Darlie's mother – "She had bruises up and down her arm, solid bruises".

Leeza Gibbons – "How do you believe she got the bruises?"

Juror - "I believe that Devon kicked the crap out of her. (Applause)

Sarilda – "Rena, you're going to have to be held accountable for that".

Juror - "He has a wound, he has a wound on his butt. Do you understand that? The only way he is going to get a bruise on his butt when he's being stabbed in the chest is if he has his feet in the air."

Juror - "HE FOUGHT FOR HIS LIFE". (More applause).

Darlie's mother – "He's not that kind of person Rena".

Sarilda - "You will be held responsible when you die. Believe me Rena, you will be held responsible."

Darlie's mother – "He weighs forty pounds".

The juror continued to answer the questions. "We hoped that she wasn't guilty. We were hoping to go in there and find her not guilty. We don't want to see a mother do that."

Q. What was it that persuaded you the most?

Juror - "There isn't one thing or another thing. I mean that videotape is pretty devastating and yes we watched it a lot."

Leeza Gibbons asked her producer to play the videotape of Darlie's party at the cemetery then asked Darin a very simple question that he evidently didn't know the answer to. "And Darin, this was your son's birthday?"

Darin didn't answer.

So, Darlie senior jumped right in and answered the question for him.

Then Leeza Gibbons said that the videotape was asked to be seen time and time again by the jury. Suddenly Darin found his voice.

"That's just because they were smart enough to push "play" and "rewind".

Referencing the videotape from the party just eight days after Darlie murdered her children the juror said, "She didn't cry. She smiled and she snapped her gum and she laughed."

Darlie's mother – "And she was on a lot of medications".

Juror – "I don't care what medications she was on".

Darlie's mother - "Maybe you should be on some."

Sarilda – "I'm telling you Rena".

The party at the cemetery was just eight days after her children were murdered but in just eight days Darlie already seemed to not have a care in the world. Since her conviction her mother and her husband claimed she was almost killed in the attack that she supposedly slept through. Yet the doctor said she could have been released from the hospital after just one day. He allowed her to stay an extra day to help protect her from the reporters.

When she was released from the hospital she went to the police station and gave her written statement. Then she went on to the funeral home and spent time with family members. The following day the family held the funeral for Devon and Damon Routier. Then just four days later Darlie was partying at the cemetery and giving a lengthy on camera interview to the reporter the family invited to the event.

Four days later Darlie went to the police station again for what would be her final police interview. As she spoke with the police investigator she said, "If I did kill my children I don't remember it".

Finally, Darlie was placed under arrest and charged with murdering Devon and Damon Routier.

Then suddenly, after getting arrested, Darlie was able to cry. For twelve days Darlie hadn't publicly shown any sadness over losing her children. But losing her freedom was altogether different. She cried, and she cried, and she cried some more. Evidently the medication excuse went out the window as the meds the "family" said kept her from crying must have worn off on the day of her arrest.

Before her arrest, she appeared to be downright happy. She had even been seen jumping up and down and clapping her hands shortly after the murders right in the front yard of their home where her sons were so brutally attacked just a few days earlier. Strangers had created a makeshift memorial for Devon and Damon where they left cards and stuffed animals in their memory. Darlie and Darin came by to pick up the stuffed animals and as Darin tossed them one by one into the car Darlie kicked, and hollered, and cheered him on as if she was trying out for the high school cheerleading squad.

Within just days of the murders Darlie and one of her friends went inside the house. Her friend was worried that the experience might be devastating for Darlie. But it wasn't. Darlie's focus wasn't on losing her children. Instead she sounded angry about how much money it would cost to get the house back into shape. Once again, her focus seemed strangely focused on material things instead of the loss of her children. And once again, even though it was the first time she walked into the house since her children were murdered, Darlie didn't cry.

But when Darlie was finally arrested her smiles, and her parties, and even her plans to fix up the house all came to a screeching halt. And she cried.

Her husband would later say that he sold everything in order to pay for Darlie's defense. But if you take a closer look, the Routiers didn't really own anything to begin with. On the surface it might have appeared as if they did. They had a nice house. They had a boat. Darin drove a Jaguar. But in truth the house was mortgaged to the hilt and the Routiers were late in making their payments. Within six months of the murders the house was lost. The boat was in need of repair and was purchased with zero money down and a hefty bank loan. And the Jaguar was an older model which, like the boat, looked prettier than it ran.

The Routiers were broke, which helps explain how Darlie qualified to have a lawyer appointed to represent her who was paid by the state of Texas. Of course, by the time Darlie's trial started the money had already started flowing in from well meaning friends and even some strangers who simply couldn't fathom how any mother could be guilty of so brutally stabbing her own children. In fact, it didn't take long for Darin to put together the best defense team that other people's money could buy.

Darlie's highly skilled and experienced defense team advised her not to take the stand in her own defense. But she didn't listen. Here is just one excerpt taken from the trial transcripts of Darlie's testimony under cross-examination which shows why the prosecutor was later quoted as saying that Darlie turned out to be his best witness.

Q. Your(sic) are going to wake up when he cut your throat, aren't you? A. I have no idea, I would assume so. Q. You wouldn't sleep through that, would you? A. I don't know what happened. I would assume so, but I cannot remember. Q. Do you really think that you could have slept when the man cut your throat? A. I don't think so. Q. You couldn't have slept when you got stabbed in the arm either, could you? A. I don't think so. Q. Okay. And, if you had awakened, if you had woken up, when your children were attacked, you would have screamed, wouldn't you? A. Unless my mouth was covered. Q. Well, I mean that would -- I guess are there more than one man attacking you? A. I have no idea, sir. Q. I mean, if there was just one guy, he can only do one thing at a time, can't he? A. Well -- Q. You only saw one man, didn't you? A. I only saw one man, yes, sir. Q. Okay. Walking away from you. And if there is just one man attacking your kids, and you saw him, you would jump up and defend your children, wouldn't you? A. I would think so, but again, I cannot remember. Q. You would think you would get up? A.Yes, sir. Q. And defend your children? A. Yes, sir. Q. Don't you know you would do that? A. Yes, sir. Q. I mean, you would defend them with your life, wouldn't you? A. Yes, sir. Q. If you saw a man attacking your children, you would scream your head off, wouldn't you? A. Yes, sir, unless my mouth was covered. Q. You would scream for your husband, wouldn't you? A. Unless my mouth was covered, yes, sir. Q. You didn't have any problems screaming for him when he finally got up and came down there, did you? A. My mouth was not covered.

Darlie talked for a bit about how her mouth was torn up, whatever that was supposed to mean. The prosecutor continued questioning her.

Q. There is no way you could be prevented from defending your children, and sounding the alarm, if you had seen them being attacked? A. What do you mean -- I'm not sure I understand what you mean.

Q. Well, if you had woken up, and some man is stabbing your children, you would have tried to stop him, wouldn't you? A. Yes, sir.

Q. Okay. But you have no memory of any of that? A. No, sir. Q. You must have been beaten first, wouldn't you say? A. Sir, I have no idea. I have sat for seven months, and tried to think of every possible thing I could think of what this man did to me. Q. Okay. A. I don't remember. Q. You don't know if you were stabbed first, or you were beaten on the arms first? A. I have no idea. I don't remember. Q. And what is the description that you remember, the best description that you have of this man? A. It's not much, he was a taller man, with dark hair. Q. Okay. Let's start with that. How tall was he? A. I cannot give you an exact -- I mean, I can just tell you that he was above -- I would think above six foot."

Was Darlie asleep? Was she awake? Was she stabbed first? Did she wake up when her imaginary intruder was stabbing her children?

Darlie conveniently answered that she didn't remember. She didn't know. She didn't understand. She wasn't sure.

But Darlie does know. Darlie has seen the evidence. Two days after the murders Darlie was able to write all about how she saw a man standing near her feet. According to one of her closest friends Darlie even admitted that she did it within hours of killing her children. Then seven months later at her trial she couldn't remember.

Had Darlie actually been attacked and saw her children being killed then it makes sense she may have suffered some sort of psychotic break with no memory of what had just occurred. It makes sense that she would have gone into shock. It makes sense that her pulse rate would have sky rocketed or that her blood pressure would have been extremely high. It makes sense that Darlie would have been shaking, or crying, or hysterical at the scene of the crime.

But Darlie's vital signs were normal. She wasn't shaking. She wasn't crying. She wasn't hysterical. And she had memory of what had just happened. Listen to the 911 call. Listen to the details she was clearly able to give the 911 operator. Darlie said, "I was fighting".

Then shortly after the murders her close friend claims Darlie admitted she killed her children. So her memory must have been working just fine then too.

Two days later Darlie gave even more information to the police officers. Her imaginary intruder wore a baseball cap. Darin fed the baby his bottle. She hadn't been feeling well the night before.

And then seven months later it seems Darlie suddenly became short on details when she took the stand at her trial. But that isn't how traumatic memory works. Victims remember more as time goes on, not less. Memories surface. Memories don't surface for a day or two then disappear altogether.

Darlie's stories changed. Her mother and her husband would have you believe that she was so traumatized by the incident that she has some sort of amnesia. But surely they must know better than that. And if it's true that Darlie confided in her close friend that she murdered her children then it seems pretty obvious that she would have also confided in her own mother and her husband and admitted what she had done.

But remember, we're talking about a woman who claims she was sexually abused by her stepfather beginning when she was just eight years old. We're talking about a woman who wrote in her journal about her own mother struggling to deal with the sexual abuse from Darlie's childhood. We're talking about a woman who handed her three children over to the man she accused of sexually abusing her when she was a child herself. Just three weeks before the murders Darlie's children spent the entire day with the man Darlie says was her attacker.

If that isn't denial I don't know what is. If that isn't lying, if that isn't pretending, if that isn't the most glaring example ever of faking it through life and pretending that everything is just fine then I don't know what is.

Darlie said the first time she was sexually molested she was just eight years old. The first time. How many times did he sexually abuse her? How many years did she suffer as a child while her mother chose to stay married to the man who was sexually abusing her daughter?

If it's true, if Darlie suffered childhood sexual abuse, then consider how the night of the murders may have happened. Darlie admits she and Darin "had words" before he finally went upstairs to go to bed at 1:00 a.m. What if Darin told Darlie he wanted a divorce? What if Darlie was upset when she went to sleep? What if Darlie was also suffering from some sort of premenstrual syndrome? Just four weeks earlier Darlie had written a suicide note to her children. "Dear Devon, Damon, and Drake, forgive me for what I'm about to do". Then once her period started a couple of days later she felt normal and happy again. Darin says he had become angry with her for how she was feeling that day one month before the murders and that they never spoke of it again.

Well maybe they should have. Maybe once her period started and she felt better they should have spoken with her doctor about her tearfulness and thoughts of suicide. But that's not how families work who are heavy into denial. They smile. They lie. They keep moving forward worrying only about how they appear to others. And when they are triggered by stress or seasons or people or experiences, and when their traumatic memories begin to surface, and the memories begin to flood their conscious minds, they will often lie even more, and pretend even more, and focus even more on how they appear to others.

Trauma Memory

Trauma memories expand. A victim may have little to no memory of a traumatic incident. Then over time they may remember more. Traumatic memory does not work the other way. A victim does not remember everything then start to lose bits and pieces of what they remembered at first.

The trauma of what occurred in her home the night her children were murdered was in her memory when she told her close friend that she murdered her children. The trauma of what happened when she murdered her children was fresh in her mind when she staged the crime scene to try to make it look like an intruder had attacked her and her children. The trauma memory did not suddenly disappear. But perhaps her memory of the lies she told to different people did.

Now take a look at the traumatic memories of being sexually molested when she was a child.

What if those memories were just beginning to surface?

What if having contact with the man she claims sexually molested her as a child stirred up even more memories of the sexual abuse from her childhood?

And what if the emotional and physical stressors in her life as an adult combined with those traumatic memories from her childhood created the perfect storm?

Theory of Repressed Memory of Childhood Sexual Abuse

Consider this hypothetical scenario specific to the theory of repressed memory of childhood sexual abuse. Darlie and Darin fought. They decided to divorce. They argued about bills. They argued over custody. Perhaps they even argued about whether Darin was hitting on her kid sister. Maybe that's the real reason that Dana had to suddenly leave the Routier home.

So Darin laughs at Darlie, tells her she's crazy, tells her he's done, that he'll be taking custody of their children and she can go get a job and support herself for once in her life.

He walks up the stairs. As he's walking up the stairs he's laughing at Darlie. She screams at him that she'll destroy him and he tells her to go to hell.

And she does.

Darlie is two days away from her period and feeling just as miserable as she felt one month earlier when she wrote her suicide note. She wasn't feeling well. She had already been angry and upset earlier in the day and spent most of her time slamming cupboard doors and sharpening her knives. That's right. I've been told by one of Darlie's closest friends that Darlie was very angry in the afternoon before she murdered her children. The car mechanic called and for some reason that call set her off.

My hunch is that the car mechanic had tried to reach Darin at the shop and when he couldn't reach him there he called the house. Then when Darlie learned that Darin wasn't at the shop I think she called for herself and found out that Darin and her kid sister Dana had taken off work that afternoon. Together.

The boys stayed outside. Devon stayed over at his friend's house and Damon rode his bike around the neighborhood. When the housekeeper's daughter arrived to pick her mom up, after working all day at Darin's shop, she saw that Darin and Dana had still not shown up at the house. Where were they all afternoon? And why weren't they home yet?

According to the housekeeper once Darlie got the call from the car mechanic she was mad. She was slamming cupboard doors. And yes, she was sharpening her knives. When Devon called and pleaded to be able to have dinner and spend the night at his friend's house, Darlie told him no. When little Damon begged the housekeeper's daughter to please take him home with her, Darlie said no.

So by the time Darlie and Darin "had words" and Darin went up to bed Darlie was already a mess. What if Darlie accused Darin of hitting on her kid sister? What if Dana got the heck out of there fast once Darlie and Darin started fighting about it? Why exactly did Dana suddenly have to leave? Was it Dana's choice? Or was it really Darlie who wanted her to leave?

When Darin got back to the house Darlie was right on the sofa where she had already spent the better part of the evening and where she would continue to sit for the next three hours straight while he and Darlie "had words".

And when he finally did go up those stairs at 1:00 a.m. Darlie planned to sleep right on that sofa too. She would later say that she was such a light sleeper that it was difficult for her to get a good night's sleep up by the baby's crib. But of course if Darlie was such a light sleeper then her excuse for sleeping on the sofa doesn't work very well when she is simultaneously trying to convince the police detectives that she slept through her children being attacked within just a few feet of where she was supposedly sleeping.

So, Darin tells her to go to hell and Darlie thinks to herself she's already there. And just who the hell does he think he is to speak to her that way? How dare he ridicule her or threaten to take custody of their children? What a bastard. She'll show him. He'll be sorry for how he has treated her.

Darlie is furious. She hates him. She just hates him. Pure and simple she hates the man she thought that she once loved.

Darlie feels like her head is ready to explode. How dare he threaten to take her children? How dare he laugh at her? How dare he spend the entire afternoon alone with her kid sister?

Men, they're all alike, Darlie thinks to herself. Darin is no better than the bastard who sexually abused her when she was a child. And the scariest part for Darlie that night during their fight would have been knowing that Darin's mother probably would take her children if Darlie and Darin ever got divorced.

Darlie knew she had problems. She knew that Darin and his family would fight for those kids and insist that Darlie get help. And that's exactly what she told Darin's employee who kept telling her to get help. It wouldn't look good in a custody battle down the road if she had to leave her kids with her mother-in-law for awhile while she got the help she needed.

Dammit, that bastard. No wonder she felt crazy all the time. No wonder she would spend days in a row not being able to get out of bed. No wonder she cried. No wonder she felt so miserable. No wonder she hated what she saw when she looked in the mirror. It was all Darin's fault. Well, she would show him.

She would call a lawyer first thing in the morning and fight for custody of those kids. There was no way in hell she was going to let Darin ruin her life. He could pay for her and for their kids. He could keep the promises he made to her the day they got married. That's why she draped her wedding dress over the chair while he was taking Dana to her boyfriend's apartment. So when he got back to the house she could put a total guilt trip on him. Darin took the best years of her life. And it was time for him to pay for what he took from her.

Dammit, Darin was no better than her mother's second husband, the man Darlie said sexually abused her when she was a child. Dana is just a kid. And Darin had damn well better not have touched her.

As Darlie begins to fall asleep she thinks about how much she hates the man who hurt her when she was a little girl. And she realizes she hates her mother too for not protecting her. But she wasn't weak like her mother. She was going to stand up to Darin and she was going to win.

Darlie starts to fall asleep but she is so full of anger she can barely breathe. She exhales slowly and tries to force herself to go to sleep. She has a long day ahead of her tomorrow. She has to see a lawyer fast and fight like hell for custody of those kids.

No man is going to use her like this. No man is going to abandon her. No man is going to tell her to get the hell out of her own house. She'll show him. She'll take him to the cleaners. She'll own him by the time this is through. She'll make him sorry that he ever fell in love with her in the first place.

That bastard. That ignorant bastard. He thinks he's getting custody of the kids but she'll show him. She'll show him that she's the one in control. Those kids are her kids. And he will pay for her and for her kids. He'll pay for threatening her. He'll pay for abandoning her. And he'll pay for ever thinking that she would take his threats lying down. He's about to find out just how evil she can be.

Darlie began to feel a little better once she decided to find a lawyer and start the divorce the very next day. She went to sleep knowing that she was about to enter into serious battle with Darin. And she was ready. She was ready to win. She'd show him. He'd be groveling at her feet in no time. And when he does Darlie will shut him down flat. She didn't need him. She didn't want him. She didn't love him anymore. In fact, she hated him. It was time to hurt him as much as he had hurt her.

In her anger, Darlie drifted off to sleep.

And soon her nightmare began.

People who theorize that Darlie killed her children in spousal revenge believe that at this point in the scenario Darlie went directly to the kitchen, grabbed a knife from her knife collection, and proceeded to murder her children. People who believe in the spousal revenge filicide theory say that Darlie probably decided right then and there that she was going to kill her children in order to destroy Darin.

But I don't think that's necessarily how it happened. In my opinion, I think there is a strong possibility that Darlie actually did fall asleep after Darin went up the stairs to go to bed at 1:00 a.m.

In my opinion she was very angry when she fell asleep. I think she was stressed beyond her ability to cope. They were broke. She was stuck home with the kids. They had a couple of big vacations planned and not even enough money in their checking account to pay their bills.

I think Darlie suspected her husband and sister of having an affair. And I think it triggered something inside her about when she was sexually abused when she was a child.

Remember her sister was just fifteen years old. And Darlie was very close to her sister. She was very protective of her sister and when she could no longer stay at her mother's house then Darlie wanted her sister to move right in with her.

Remember also that Darlie had just allowed the man she said sexually abused her to take her children for the day just a few weeks before the murders.

I think Darlie was stressed and I think she was triggered by having close contact with the man she says sexually abused her when she was a child. And it's just my hunch but in my opinion the man Darlie described to the police as being the intruder was probably her stepdad.

Being stressed and triggered I think as soon as Darlie fell asleep the memories of the sexual abuse she says she suffered through when she was a child came flooding to the surface from her subconscious mind.

So, at some point after 1:00 a.m., I think Darlie fell asleep in a fit of anger. Then I think Darlie had a nightmare like so many other adult survivors of childhood sexual abuse have. In her nightmare she is being attacked by her abuser. She sees him standing over her. She knows what he's there for. She hates him. She hates how he hurts her. She hates her mother for not protecting her. She hates feeling so vulnerable and defenseless.

But this nightmare is different. She is an adult now. And she's angry. She's not going to allow her abuser to hurt her ever again. She's going to destroy her abuser and make him pay for every time he has hurt her.

In her nightmare, she sees herself taking a knife from her kitchen. She stabs her attacker. She stabs him hard, again and again. And she stabs her mother too. How dare she allow the abuse to happen? So she hates her mother too for not protecting her when she was young. She stabs, and she stabs, and she stabs and each time she swings that knife back and stabs again it counts for each time her abusive stepfather sexually molested her.

Then suddenly her nightmare comes to an end. She won the fight. She killed her attacker. He's dead. And her mother is too. No more fake smiles. No more pretending. No more lies. No more fears of falling asleep then seeing her stepfather standing near her feet staring at her when she opens her eyes in the middle of the night.

Finally Darlie feels free. And safe. And happy.

And Darlie feels exhausted too. Depleted. And suddenly all alone.

But in her nightmare Darlie realizes she isn't angry anymore. She's tired but happy just the same. She looks around and decides it's time to clean her house. She likes her house to be spotless. She likes her carpets to be white. She sees that she has a lot of work to do.

Suddenly Darlie opens her eyes.

And she sees that her living nightmare has just begun.

Darlie sees that lying before her on the floor isn't the body of the woman who didn't protect her when she was young.

He is her child.

She looks over and sees that the other body lying on the floor isn't the man who she has accused of sexually molesting her when she was just a little girl.

He is her younger son.

Darlie realizes what she has done. In her rage, in her nightmare, it wasn't her mother and stepfather she was stabbing. She was actually stabbing her own children.

Darlie doesn't scream. She doesn't dial 911. She doesn't kill herself like she had considered doing just one month before.

Instead, in a frenzy, she tries to make it look like somebody else killed her children. She tosses a wine glass to the floor. She carefully lays the coffee table on its side. She has to get rid of the knife so she takes a sock from the laundry room, wipes the handle clean then puts her hand in the sock so her fingerprints won't be on the knife. Darlie doesn't know that the handles of her knife set are hard to ever get prints from. So she's very careful to cover her hand with the sock. She takes the knife outside and drops it down the sewer drain. She carefully takes the sock off her hand and drops that down the sewer drain too not realizing that it fell to the side. Darlie goes back inside and looks around. Everything looked just right. But there was just one problem. She knew she had to be injured too.

So she stood at the kitchen sink and carefully tried to stab herself on the arm. She realized she didn't feel a thing. She was ready. So she lifted her chin and carefully sliced near her own throat. She had the towel ready. She knew to apply pressure to her wounds.

Then it happened. She heard her younger son say "Mommy". She closed her eyes and held on to the counter. She could remember now. She saw him looking right at her when she was stabbing him. She heard him say "Mommy" as he looked right into her eyes. She heard it again. But wait. This wasn't just a memory.

Her son was still alive! Was he calling for her? Or was he trying to say that it was her who stabbed him? Darlie took another knife from her knife block. She walked into the family room. And after she stabbed both of her sons again, Darlie screamed.

Her husband came running down the stairs. He tried to save their children while Darlie dialed 911.

In Defense of Darlie

If Darlie is guilty of killing her children in my opinion she is not the only person to blame. Darlie needed help long before the murders. While her husband and her mother say that she was "normal" or that she never had any problems, the fact is that Darlie needed help and neither one of them were willing to admit it.

One month, one menstrual cycle, before Darlie murdered her children she almost killed herself. Previous to that day she had been staying in bed for hours on end. She was crying. She was miserable. She needed help. But the way her husband explained it he became angry with her for how she was feeling. Darlie herself was concerned about getting help because if her kids needed to stay with her mother-in-law for awhile Darlie said that wouldn't look good in a custody battle down the road. Darin's employee, Basia, who was Darlie's maid of honor when Darin and Darlie got married pleaded with both Darin and Darlie to get the help Darlie needed. And they refused.

Why were the Routiers behind on their bills? According to Darin he made plenty of money. So why were they broke?

Why was Darlie put on a diet pill when she was only twelve pounds overweight?

Why was Darlie planning a big vacation to Mexico with her girlfriend when she didn't even have a car to drive or enough money to pay their monthly bills on time?

Why did Darin and Dana leave work early in the day and stay gone together all afternoon?

And when Darlie was so stressed out and upset why on earth did her mother allow her kid sister to move right in. She was fifteen years old and should not have been Darlie's responsibility.

Once Darlie was arrested why didn't her mother and her husband own up to the problems she had been having? Didn't they realize that the best way to help her would have been to admit the problems she was having before the murders?

Didn't they realize that it was time to stop the lies about how she was acting?

Didn't they realize that she needed them to protect her?

Over and over again Darlie went to the police station and spoke with the detectives without a lawyer by her side. Her mother said that finally Darlie's grandpa said that maybe it wasn't a good idea to keep talking to the police detectives with having a lawyer with her. But Darlie and her husband insisted that she didn't need a lawyer.

Why?

Why didn't either one of them make one quick phone call and hire the best lawyer they could find? When they were in trouble for violating a gag order they sure found a good lawyer in a hurry. So why didn't they do the same for Darlie?

When Darlie was prancing around the neighborhood shortly after the murders, where were her husband and her mother? She listened to them. She trusted them. If they had told her to stay inside and not to be gallivanting around she would have obeyed them.

And why on earth did her husband and her mother both take part in the party at the cemetery? Surely they saw how Darlie was acting. And they knew the cameras were rolling.

Who was protecting Darlie?

Who has ever protected Darlie?

Instead they both insist that Darlie did not murder her children. They both give the interviews, and talk and talk and talk about what a great mother Darlie is. But Darlie isn't a great mother.

Darlie was known for yelling at her young children to "get the hell out of the house". Her mother and her husband say that Darlie's house was the house where all of the neighborhood children congregated. But like the prosecutor said, Darlie was no June Cleaver. And if the neighborhood kids were always at her house then why is it that the one day there is evidence of where the children were her own children appear to have been avoiding her. In fact they both pleaded to be able to stay somewhere else the night she murdered them.

Darlie's mom said that Darlie made a big dinner for the boys the evening before they were murdered. In fact Darlie sat her children at a separate table in the kitchen and gave them a bowl of chicken soup.

Darlie's husband said that she was a room mother at their son's school and that she helped out at school a lot. Yet not one parent from the school stepped up in defense of Darlie.

And once Darlie was arrested who was protecting her then? Writing letters back and forth while she was in jail surely put her at risk. And feeding her stories with suspect after suspect simply helped to make her look like a liar and a fool when she took the witness stand.

That family should have had a lawyer by Darlie's side when she was still in the hospital. When the detectives showed up to question her that family should have refused to allow them anywhere near. And when the police wanted Darlie to go directly to the police station when she was released from the hospital, that family should have said no. They should have said they have two young boys to mourn and after the funeral when Darlie was in better shape to talk then they would bring her in to speak with the police detectives then.

When they hired Darlie's new lawyer they should have told him everything they knew. If it's true there was some kind of insurance scam set up then obviously they should have been honest with Darlie's lawyer right from the start. If it's true there was a black car seen in the neighborhood then they should have used some of the money they raised to pay for private investigators. Because it sure seems that if they had been honest, if they had told her lawyer how Darlie had changed so much in recent months, how she cried, how she struggled to keep the house clean, how she yelled at the kids, and at her husband, then maybe the lawyer could have helped her. Maybe not during the trial but at least during the sentencing phase of the trial.

And when her lawyers told her not to testify, but she insisted on it anyway, where was her family then? Why on earth didn't they insist that she keep her mouth shut?

I don't believe that her mother and her husband believed she was innocent. Ever. I believe they knew from the start that Darlie killed her children.

And like families do who are highly skilled in keeping up the appearances and pretending away the evil that lurks within, I think her family chose to keep right on lying about what had gone on in that family, not only the night of the murders, but all during Darlie's life.

Why on earth was Darlie handing her children over for the day to the man who she says had started sexually abusing her when she was just eight years old? Why did it take ten years for her mother to divorce her abuser? Why when Darlie and Darin got married did she not have a friend from high school standing up beside her? Instead she chose one of Darin's co-workers as her maid of honor. Why? Did she have any friends from high school? Was Darlie ever allowed to have a childhood?

Darlie Routier is on death row. Her appeals are running out. Her husband has divorced her and moved on with his life. Her mother, bless her heart, is still fighting the fight, but she is fighting it alone. Darlie's father, sisters, aunts and uncles, cousins, etc. are all noticeably silent on social media. In their place is a handful of "friends" who vehemently deny Darlie's guilt.

They insult, they ridicule, they threaten, and they harass people on social media who realize Darlie is guilty of capital murder. Yes, the jury got it right. But her few supporters refuse to discuss the details of the case. Instead they swear and they bully and they lie.

I do not believe in the death penalty. However, the state of Texas does. And soon Darlie will be executed if her supporters don't start telling the truth about what happened to two sweet little innocent boys on June 6, 1996.

I don't know if it would do any good but it sure seems like it would be worth a try to own up to what happened. Own up to the problems Darlie was having. Learn from her mistakes. Ask Darlie questions and learn about the suffering that adult survivors of childhood sexual abuse endure.

Because that's about the only good it seems that can come from this tragedy. Nothing will bring Devon and Damon back or give Darlie back the last twenty years of her life. But if Darlie can be honest and if she can explain how she was feeling and how she was thinking and how she was shocked when she opened her eyes then she can surely help other young women and hopefully help keep them from the dangers that she and Devon and Damon faced.

Look at Susan Smith. Look at Andrea Yates. Susan Smith was sexually molested too. And I don't know if Andrea Yates was but I wouldn't be surprised to hear it. Susan Smith told the truth. And she didn't get the death penalty. Andrea Yates told the truth and she was able to get the help she needed.

Mothers who kill their own children have serious issues going on. Diane Downs said that she was sexually molested by her father too. And like Susan Smith she was recently rejected by her lover. Casey Anthony was found not guilty of killing her daughter but even at her trial it came out that she was sexually molested too.

Until women who kill their children are honest and open about exactly what happened and what went through their minds at the time of the murders then younger women cannot be helped. Families like Darlie's will continue to suffer as they publicly insist she is innocent regardless of the evidence that proves them wrong.

Nothing is learned. Nobody is helped. Women will continue to suffer. And children will continue to be killed. In the United States alone there are an estimated 250 children dying each year who are murdered by the one person they should be able to trust the most; their own mother.

Darlie and her mother have an opportunity to help others. But the only way they can help others is if they will be honest about what happened to Darlie when she was young. The only way they can help others is if they'll be honest about how miserable Darlie felt long before the murders. The only way they can help others is if they face the facts about what happened on June 6, 1996.

Younger women need to know how Darlie felt. They need to know what Darlie was thinking. They need to hear how Darlie suffered because young women who were sexually abused when they were children are suffering too.

Doctors and counselors and psychologists and ministers and nurses and friends need to be able to read about Darlie's experiences. The issue of traumatic memory following childhood sexual abuse is serious and prevalent in our society but is rarely discussed or understood.

Darlie and her mother can help bring the issue of childhood sexual abuse out in the open. And if her story can save even just one little boy from being killed by his mother then their willingness to come forward is worth it.

In one of Darlie's mother's interviews she talks about the time one of her precious grandsons wrapped up a slinky and gave it to her at Christmas time. She cries when she tells this story and her story is so heartbreaking that anyone who hears it cries right along with her as they listen to her speak with such love and sadness in her voice. Clearly, her heart was broken the morning she got the call at 3:00 a.m. telling her that poor little Devon and Damon were dead.

But she doesn't stick with the sadness. She turns on a dime and insists that her daughter was targeted by an overzealous criminal justice system. She says the nurses lied on the stand, the police officers were liars too. The prosecutors were out to get her daughter. The judge wasn't being fair when he switched the location of the trial. In fact, it was Darlie who requested the change of venue but that little detail gets lost in the tirade.

Darlie's mother says that her daughter was convicted because of the silly string video.

But she wasn't convicted because of the silly string video. Darlie was convicted of capital murder because she is guilty as sin. And the evidence proves it.

Just think if her mother could give an interview where she starts off with her story about the Christmas gift from her precious grandson. She would have every mom and grandma and sister and friend hanging on her every word. Then imagine that instead of switching into high gear about how rotten the criminal justice system is she could instead talk about how she didn't realize what was happening with her daughter when she was so miserable right before the murders. Or maybe she could talk about how she didn't realize that her daughter was being sexually abused when she was a child.

Maybe Darlie's mom could talk about how looking back she realizes there were signs that she wishes now she had taken more seriously. Or maybe she can talk about how her daughter told her that she was being abused but maybe she didn't believe her at the time.

Maybe Darlie's mom could give an interview about how she encouraged Darlie to have contact with her abuser without knowing the risks to Darlie's well-being that having contact with her abuser could bring.

Or maybe Darlie's mom could give an interview about how she wishes with all her heart that she would have insisted Darlie get professional help just one month before the murders when she contemplated committing suicide.

Darlie's mom is an excellent speaker. And her story is one which women want to hear.

But women want to hear the real story. The truth. The heartache of knowing her daughter was sexually abused and the guilt for not having protected her when she was younger. If Darlie's mom will speak out on the impact childhood sexual abuse had on her daughter's life, and on her life, and on the lives of her other children and her grandchildren then she can use the experience of losing her grandsons and make something good come of it.

The same holds true for Darlie. She is sitting on death row. Her execution date must be coming soon considering she has been sitting on death row for twenty years already. Darlie is an excellent speaker just like her mother. Both women are intelligent and articulate. Both women have so much to share that could be helpful for other women who are also struggling.

Of course, because Darlie is represented by attorneys then anything either woman has to say should be approved by Darlie's lawyers first. But just imagine if they are granted permission to speak. To speak fully, and truthfully, and completely about what happened and about what they know now about the experiences Darlie suffered through in her life.

Instead of calling everyone else on the planet a liar they should both stop and look in a mirror and realize to what extent the two of them have failed to be honest even if only with themselves. Face the truth. Face the facts. Refuse to lie. Refuse to pretend any longer.

Over and over again Darlie and her mother have claimed that she was convicted because of the silly string video. But Darlie wasn't convicted because of silly string. She was convicted because the direct physical evidence clearly showed she is guilty of capital murder.

Yes Darlie is guilty. And it's time for Darlie and her mother to both admit it.

Darlie is guilty but she is not the only person to blame for what happened in the Routier home on June 6, 1996. The list is long of people who looked the other way when Darlie was showing signs of trouble. The list is long of people who could have helped Darlie if only they knew how. The list is long of people who truly had no clue how to help or even that help was needed in the first place. The list is long of people who expected Darlie to associate with the man who she claimed started sexually abusing her when she was just eight years old.

Darlie and her mother could both help to right so many wrongs. Of course, nothing could ever take away what Darlie did but from the tragedy she and her mother could use their voices to reach out to other moms and grammies and really help those in need. Women are suffering, moms are struggling, and little girls are continuing to be sexually molested and growing to become very angry young women.

Darlie and her mother are both highly skilled at giving interviews. With her lawyer's permission it's time for both of them to speak the truth. If they still want to claim she did not murder her children, if they are both insistent on claiming she is innocent, then hopefully they can at least speak out on childhood sexual abuse and how the pain continued right on throughout Darlie's life.

Maybe that would be a good starting point for both women. Maybe they could begin to face the impact the sexual abuse had on Darlie when she was in her twenties. Maybe that will be the only way they can both come to grips with what Darlie did to her children.

Then hopefully they will be able to make sense of what happened. Maybe they'll be able to understand that repressed memories of childhood sexual abuse are very powerful once they emerge from the subconscious mind. Maybe they can learn how associating with the abuser can be dangerous to a young woman's well-being.

Maybe they can learn about traumatic memory and how it impacts adult survivors on every level of their being. Maybe they can put together a time line and realize that the stressors that Darlie was facing in all areas of her life combined with the expectation that she allow her abuser in her home and near her own children created the perfect storm.

And maybe, just maybe, they can both learn to accept that what Darlie did made sense after all. I'm not saying what she did was right or normal or okay in any way. What Darlie did was horrible. But maybe if they could both realize how it happened or why it happened they could understand that in the end there were three victims in the Routier tragedy. Devon and Damon and their mother Darlie too.

Darlie needed help. She needed protection. She needed someone to put their arms around her and tell her she was safe and loved and perfect just the way she was. She didn't need make-up or a boob job or diet pills or new clothes to be safe and loved and protected.

And she certainly did not need to associate with the person she claimed had sexually abused her when she was a child.

Once Darlie and her mom can both face the truth, and with the permission of Darlie's lawyers, I hope they speak out in truth and in kindness to help other adult survivors of childhood sexual abuse. Darlie and her mother both have so much to offer other women. But until they do face the facts and admit the truth they really aren't helping anyone, not even themselves.

When people speak up on social media and insist that the evidence proves Darlie is guilty of killing her children, her mother and her mother's fb friends go on the attack. That simply needs to stop. It doesn't help anyone suddenly think that Darlie isn't guilty. All that behavior does is convince them even more that Darlie surely must be right where she belongs.

But if Darlie could be honest and if she could write about the abuse she says she suffered as a child and how it affected her when she was a mother herself then just think of the support she would get. If Darlie's mother could write about how she maybe didn't know or realize that her daughter was being hurt, or maybe she did know but she somehow didn't feel she could get out or she didn't know how to protect her at the time, then just think of the support she would also get right along with her daughter.

In Texas, when someone is convicted of capital murder they get the death penalty. So of course Darlie's lawyers have been working hard on her appeals. And anything Darlie says or does should certainly be only on the advice of her lawyers. But just think if they do allow her to speak the truth of what happened on June 6, 1996 in the Routier home.

Just think if suddenly Darlie's story is made known and it all comes down to the impact that being sexually abused as a young girl had on her later in life.

Darlie's mom says that her doctors found Darlie to be normal. But look at the evidence. Dig in. Tell the truth about what was happening in Darlie's world before the murders. Tell the truth about the stress she was under and her reactions to it. Tell the truth about whatever kind of diet pills she was on. Research. Explore. Ask questions.

Was the diet pill Darlie was taking later found to cause aggressive behaviors? Was the diet pill known to cause altered thinking or even nightmares?

Was Darlie eating properly? Was Darlie dehydrated? Was Darlie vitamin D deficient? Was Darlie ever anorexic or bulimic?

Find out about Postpartum Psychosis. Research it. Find out why American doctors aren't taught about it in western schools. Find out how rare it is. Find out how it is so difficult to ever diagnose.

Find out about traumatic memory. Learn about the amygdala. Learn how traumatic memory is stored and then how it is triggered and what can trigger it. Learn about flooding. Learn about the dangers of allowing your abuser to be near your children when they are the same age you were when you were abused.

Learn about how the triggers can be as simple as the exhaust smell of a lawnmower or the smell of the air right after it rains. Familiar noises or foods or certain music or sights or smells can all trigger repressed memories of childhood sexual abuse. Learn about it then ask whether Darlie was first abused as a child in the month of June. Or was it exceptionally hot when she was first abused? Or was she sleeping on the floor of the family room when it first happened like Devon and Damon were the night they were murdered.

Look for the connections. Look for the triggers. Look for the possibilities of what could have led to Darlie being flooded with memories or nightmares of the abuse she suffered as a child.

Research rage. Research PMS. Research PMDD. Research the effect hormones have on our bodies when we stop breastfeeding our babies. Learn about thyroid hormones T-3 and T-4 and how fluctuations can make us feel fearful or can make us cry. Learn about estrogen and progesterone after giving birth and the importance of proper diet and nutrition.

Maybe it is too late for Darlie to be protected. Maybe it's too late for her to be saved from the death chamber in a Texas state prison. But maybe not. Maybe if she and her mother are encouraged to tell the truth and to be open and honest with the public then maybe, just maybe, there will literally be millions of women standing up to fight for Darlie's life to be spared.

I have been very vocal about the Darlie Routier case. I have been insulted and ridiculed and even threatened during a late night phone call. But I keep standing up and being vocal because I want to know the truth.

And I still struggle with how on earth it can be true that a mother would harm her own children. But the evidence against Darlie seems clear. And I believe that the evidence proves Darlie is guilty of murdering her children. But even though I believe she is guilty I don't believe she should be executed. In Darlie's case if she will be truthful then I think God does have a plan for her life which includes her being able to share what she has been through in order to help others who have also been abused.

Darlie loved her children. And she killed them. Why? What happened? Why did a mother who loved her children murder them? Why did Susan Smith strap her two little boys into their car seats then have her car go into the lake? Why did Diane Downs shoot all three of her children, murdering one, while she was out with her kids for a late night drive? And why did Andrea Yates drown her five children one by one as soon as her husband left for work?

Were these women all victims of childhood sexual abuse? And at the time of the murders were they all feeling sudden rejection from the men who they loved? Were they having regular periods? Were they taking diet pills? Was Darlie truly a victim of childhood sexual abuse? And when she and Darin had words right before she murdered their children had Darin just rejected her?

These are the questions which need to be answered if we, as women, are going to work together to help young moms who are struggling with these same issues. These are the questions which need to be answered if we, as moms, and grammies, and great-grammies too, and sisters, and aunts, and friends and neighbors, if we as women are going to say enough. We care. We're listening. We hear you. And we will do all that we can to help you and to help protect your children.

Time is running out for Darlie. But if her lawyers say that it's okay for her to tell the truth then there is a world of women who need to hear what she has to say. And when there is a world of women who hears her story and who understands what happened and why then maybe, just maybe, with our collective voice we can persuade the governor of Texas to get involved in Darlie's case.

We need to hear the truth from Darlie in order to be able to support her in her fight to live. And we need to hear the truth from her mom too who has been so vocal since Darlie was first convicted of capital murder and sent to death row. Because all Darlie's mom has to do is tell her slinky story how her precious grandson wrapped it up so messy for her and how she would give anything for a Christmas like that again to get our attention. And once she has our attention we will all benefit by hearing the truth of what really happened to Darlie and how those events surely led to the tragic night when she murdered her babies.

Snarls and insults and writing bad book reviews won't help Darlie get the help she needs. And neither will telling lies about what happened to little Devon and Damon Routier. But the slinky story, followed by the truth, the whole truth, and nothing but the truth, in my opinion, will help both Darlie and her mother gain millions of supporters worldwide who will become vocal in encouraging the state of Texas to spare Darlie's life.

Diane Downs didn't deserve to be sexually abused when she was a young girl. Susan Smith didn't deserve to be sexually abused. If Andrea Yates was sexually abused she didn't deserve to be. And when her doctor told her husband that she should not have any more children her husband should have listened. Casey Anthony didn't deserve to be sexually molested when she was young. And neither did Darlie Routier.

And each and every child who was born to one of these women deserved to have a mommy who would keep them safe.

The crime of childhood sexual abuse is one of the most despicable crimes ever committed and the ripple effects of such abuse is running rampant in our society today.

We need women like Darlie and her mom to be open and honest about what happened to Darlie when she was young. And when the truth comes out Darlie and her mom deserve to have our support.

www.ingramcontent.com/pod-product-compliance
Lightning Source LLC
Chambersburg PA
CBHW071133280526
45787CB00003B/1270

* 9 7 8 1 5 3 5 2 0 6 7 5 4 *